Stourhead
Landscape Garden

Wiltshire

Treading the Paths of Paradise

Not far from Stourhead House, the flat meadow suddenly falls away into a steep valley at a spot known as 'Paradise'. When the sun sets over the far slope, glinting off the lake and gilding the hanging woods, it feels just like that.

Here, from the 1740s Henry Hoare II created the perfect landscape garden. He dammed the stream to make a huge single lake, around which he laid out a circuit walk. As you progress round the lake, you take in a series of carefully composed views of classical and Gothic buildings set against wooded slopes. For this extraordinary achievement, Henry Hoare was justly nicknamed 'the Magnificent'.

Henry's successors have cherished his brilliant original conception, while enriching it with new planting. Specimen conifers, flowering shrubs and pelargoniums were added in the 19th century, new hybrid rhododendrons in the 20th century, so that Stourhead now has one of the most important plant collections in Britain, which has something to offer at every season.

Stourhead garden may seem like a self-contained world, but from it you can get glimpses out into the wider landscape of the estate, which combines prehistoric remains with ancient hamlets and working farms. The continuity of the estate through the centuries has given Stourhead a quality of timeless tranquillity. It offers inspiration and solace to the many thousands of visitors who come to Stourhead each year and to the local people who live and work within it.

Visitors have been welcome in the garden from the beginning, and the first guidebook was produced as early as 1800. Alda, Lady Hoare, who, with her husband, gave Stourhead to the National Trust in 1946, was quite clear: 'I love the trippers and love to see them enjoying themselves. Besides, I think one's no right to always shut a thing up, that others want to see.'

Henry Hoare 'the Magnificent', creator of the garden.

(*Right*) Henry Hoare's garden in 1775. This view takes in (*from left to right*) the Temple of Apollo, the Palladian Bridge and the Pantheon

A golden-leaved Tulip Tree towers over the island at the east end of the lake in autumn

3

A Living Work of Art
Stourhead and the Landscape Garden

Claude's idealised views of the Italian countryside inspired Stourhead's combination of classical temples and wooded landscape

(*Above right*) The garden at Prior Park near Bath was also laid out as a circular walk around a wooded valley and lake

The 18th-century landscape garden at Studley Royal in Yorkshire also combines lakes with Gothic and classical buildings

Stourhead is one of the supreme examples of the landscape garden – perhaps Britain's most important contribution to 18th-century European culture. Early in that century, British garden designers were still following the French model of straight vistas and formal flowerbeds radiating from the central axis of the house. This style found its grandest expression at Versailles and reflected the stifling formality of life in the French court. Such elaborate and unproductive gardens were extremely expensive to create and maintain, and by the 1730s they had fallen out of fashion in Britain. In 1712 the critic Joseph Addison had proposed a less expensive alternative:

Fields of corn make a pleasant prospect, and if the walks were a little taken care of that lie between them, if the natural embroidery of the meadows were helped and improved by some small additions of art … a man might make a pretty landskip of his own possessions.

Through his writings, Addison encouraged Hoare and his contemporaries to conceive their gardens as gently idealised versions of nature, which would be open to the wider countryside thanks to sunken ditches (known as ha-has) or dams, as at Stourhead. Their model was the landscape painting, and in particular the idealised views of Italy painted by Claude, Poussin and Gaspar Dughet in the 17th century. Hoare owned two large landscapes by Gaspar Dughet, which now hang in the Picture Gallery, and visualised his garden in explicitly pictorial terms: 'The view of the bridge, village and church altogether will be a charm[in]g Gasp[ar]d picture at that end of the water.' The result was the 'Picturesque' garden, which at first meant simply 'like a picture'.

Unlike many of his rivals, who were remodelling earlier formal gardens tied to an existing building, Henry Hoare inherited a house that was some way from the valley, which had never been part of his father's garden. So he could compose his garden views with all the freedom of a landscape painter working on a bare canvas. And in turn Stourhead has inspired artists ever since.

Henry Hoare compared this carefully composed view to a painting by Gaspar Dughet (view G)

The Meaning of Stourhead

The local springs that feed the lake are marked by the statue of a classical water nymph in the Grotto. This pastel was drawn by Henry Hoare II's painter friend, William Hoare of Bath

For Henry Hoare II, Alfred the Great symbolised the triumph of native arms and culture over foreign invaders

Why should a garden mean anything? Today, we prefer to enjoy gardens simply as attractive combinations of planting and landscape. But for our 18th-century ancestors, they could also have complex local, historical and political resonances. Stourhead can be understood in all these ways.

Locality

Stourhead may be a human creation, but it depends fundamentally on its position, where two steep valleys meet at Six Wells Bottom. At this natural watershed rise the springs which feed the lake and, below that, the River Stour – hence the name: Stourhead. The previous owners, the Stourtons, had taken both their name and their coat of arms from the place, and Henry Hoare II was very conscious that his garden would have been impossible without these springs. The statues of the water nymph and the river god he placed in the Grotto pay tribute to their importance.

Antiquity

In his youth, Henry Hoare II had visited Italy, where he was fascinated by the remains of classical and Renaissance Rome. He filled his garden with buildings and statues that recall these worlds. Most prominent is the Pantheon, which was based directly on a temple begun in the era of the Roman Emperor Augustus. In the early 18th century, many Britons felt that they were living through a new Augustan age of political supremacy, culture and peace. Inscriptions from the *Aeneid*, the epic poem written by

Augustus's favourite poet, Virgil, appear at key points in the garden. Virgil's hero Aeneas was celebrated as the founder of Rome, and there were even some who believed that his descendants had gone on to found Britain. In 1588 Henry Lyte of Lytes Cary, sixteen miles from Stourhead, had written a book trying to prove just this.

Inside the Pantheon is a huge statue of Hercules, a legendary hero of immense strength who was forced to undertake twelve labours. Hoare acknowledged that he was able to enjoy his tranquil garden at Stourhead only thanks to his labours in the family bank in London.

Liberty

Augustus may have brought peace to Rome, but it had been bought at the price of freedom, as Hoare and his contemporaries understood. By contrast, Britain was lucky enough to enjoy both peace and freedom at home. This happy combination was symbolised in the figure of Alfred the Great. Hoare commissioned a bust of Alfred, which still sits in the house, and built Alfred's Tower two miles to the north-west of the garden (see p.22). The inscription on the tower praises Alfred as the originator of trial by jury and 'the Founder of the English Monarchy and Liberty'. Within the garden, two Gothic buildings highlight other advantages of the British way of life over the classical world. The High Cross from Bristol's market square celebrates Britain's prosperity as a trading nation, while the old church embodies the enduring strength of the revealed Protestant religion.

Rysbrack's statue of Hercules in the Pantheon. The pose was based on a famous classical statue, and the impressive biceps on a contemporary prize-fighter

Tour of the Garden

The view down from the site of the Turkish Tent to the Pantheon (view B)

Richard Colt Hoare's Pelargonium House has recently been revived in the Walled Garden

The Gatehouse

As you walk over the modern bridge from the car-park, you can see, on your right, the castellated gatehouse, which marks the main entrance to the house. It is all that survives of the Stourtons' old house, but was moved to its present position by Richard Colt Hoare in 1799.

The Walled Garden

You walk through the old Walled Garden, which once supplied fruit and vegetables to the house. The highlight today is the Pelargonium House, a Victorian peach-house re-erected here in 1998 to grow pelargoniums, which Richard Colt Hoare had first introduced to Stourhead in the early 19th century, when they were being imported from South Africa in large numbers. By 1821 Colt Hoare owned over 600 species, including *P. tricolor*, *echinatum* and *grandiflorum*, and was creating more hybrids himself. Such was the fame of his collection that one subspecies was named after him. The cost of re-creating the Pelargonium House was met by the Kensington and Chelsea Association of the National Trust.

The Stableyard and Ice-house

The tarmac road up to the house takes you past the stableyard on the left, which probably occupies the site of the old Stourton Manor, which Henry Hoare I demolished when he built his new house. On your right are some 400–500-year-old Sweet Chestnuts, which may have once lined the drive to Stourton Manor. *Turn left into the trees behind the stables.*

On the lawn in front of you is an Indian Bean Tree (*Catalpa bignonioïdes*). This was introduced to Britain in the early 18th century, with specimens planted at Stourhead from 1791.

Hidden in the trees on the left is the ice-house, which, in the days before fridges, would have provided ice for the

The obelisk marks the end of the Fir Walk

kitchen through the summer. Ice would be cut from the frozen lake and laid in this cool and well-insulated interior between layers of straw. Ice in summer was one of the luxuries that Henry Hoare II felt he had earned by his hard work.

The Obelisk

The obelisk is first visible from the west front of the house across Great Oar Meadow. Obelisks originate in ancient Egypt, where they symbolised the sun, so they make appropriate features for a garden. The Romans first used them as garden ornaments, and the idea was revived in the Renaissance. More modest versions appear in Britain in the 16th century on garden walls like those at Montacute in Somerset.

Henry Hoare II erected the first obelisk in 1746 to close his Fir Walk. By 1839 it had decayed and had to be replaced in Bath stone. Further restoration was needed in 1853 after it was struck by lightning. At the end of the lawn is a large Tulip Tree, planted by Colt Hoare around 1800. Its leaves turn a wonderful butter yellow in autumn.

The Fir Walk

This was Henry Hoare II's first tentative addition to the garden. Laid out in the 1730s, it offered a traditional formal vista along the ridge above the south side of the valley. In 1757 the novelist Samuel Richardson praised the 'softest mossy turf, bordered on each side by stately Scotch Firs'. Richard Colt Hoare disliked his grandfather's conifers, which he felt interfered with the outline of the deciduous woodland, and removed many of them.

The gatehouse is all that remains of the Stourtons' earlier house

9

Looking west over the lake from Six Wells Bottom. The obelisk is on the horizon at the left. Watercolour by Francis Nicholson, about 1813

A Japanese maple below the Shades at the eastern end of the lake

The view from the Temple of Flora to the Temple of Apollo

Turn left when you reach the junction on the lower path beside the lake, if you want to see the Temple of Flora close up. The best view of it is from the Pantheon on the other side of the lake (see p.14).

The Temple of Flora

Here, above a natural spring known as Paradise Well, Henry Hoare II erected his first garden building in 1744–6 to designs by his favourite architect, Henry Flitcroft. The temple was inspired by one in the famous garden created by the Roman writer Pliny and is dedicated to the Roman goddess of flowers and spring. Over the door is an inscription taken from Virgil's *Aeneid*: *'Procul, O procul este, profani'* ('Keep away, anyone profane, keep away'). These are the solemn words spoken by the Cumaean Sybil to Aeneas as he enters

the Underworld. Hoare is asking you to enter his garden in the right spirit. The temple is surrounded by evergreen shrubs, principally laurel, yew and rhododendron, which are meant to evoke this serious mood.

Retrace your steps back to the lakeside path.

The Shades

This is an appropriate name for the shady paths that run beneath the trees along the south side of the lake. The planting – mostly beeches and other deciduous trees, but interspersed with the occasional fir – reaches down to the water's edge in places, with open glades elsewhere so that you can enjoy the views over the lake, as Colt Hoare intended.

Originally, the walk around the long eastern neck of the lake was rather shorter, as you were meant to cross it by a 100 foot-wide oak bridge just beyond the island. The bridge was replaced by a ferry in 1798, and later the walk was extended further round the lake, passing between Lily Lake and Diana's Basin, a still and dark pool.

Six Wells Bottom

The streams which feed the garden start here. For a moment, you get a glimpse of the world beyond the garden. From the dam, you can look east into an open, pastoral valley which formed part of an enclosed deer-park before the 18th century. On either side are wooded slopes, known – for obvious reasons – as Sunny and Shady Hangings. They reflect 18th-century landscapers' fascination with light and shade.

The Temple of Flora is dedicated to the Roman goddess of flowers and spring

The view out over the lake from the Grotto

The 'Nymph of the Grot' sleeps beside the cold bath, which is fed by natural springs

(*Right*) Henry Cheere's lead statue of a classical river god, who points visitors on their way towards the Pantheon

12

The North Bank

As you walk back up through the trees along the north side of the lake, the wider garden is temporarily lost from view. This puts one in the right mood for the Grotto, 'lost in a wood', as Horace Walpole described it in 1762.

The Grotto

Grottoes were popular in Italian Renaissance gardens, as a place of cool retreat from summer heat. The poet Alexander Pope popularised them in Britain with the grotto in his garden at Twickenham. However, Dr Johnson wondered whether grottoes were really suitable for the English climate, suggesting that they would make 'a pretty cool summer habitation for a toad'.

The rockwork around the outside of the Grotto is planted with shade-loving ferns and native woodland plants. Inside is a circular domed chamber lined with a local 'rustic' limestone and tufa, which Henry Hoare imported from Italy. For the Romans, such places were shrines to the gods and the home of water nymphs ('*Nympharum domus*', as the inscription from Virgil's *Aeneid* above the entrance ends). Hence the statue of a sleeping nymph, which was based on a famous classical figure of Ariadne in the Vatican gardens.

According to George Eliot, she 'lies in the marble voluptuousness of her beauty, the drapery folding around her with a petal-like ease and tenderness'. On the rim of the cold bath in front of her are lines from a 15th-century Latin poem translated by Pope:

Nymph of the Grot, these sacred springs I keep
And to the Murmur of these Waters sleep;
Ah! Spare my slumbers, gently tread the cave
And drink in silence or in silence lave [wash].

During the hot summer of 1762 Henry Hoare II enjoyed cooling off here: 'A souse in that delicious bath and grot, filld with fresh magic, is Asiatick luxury'.

Like the most perfectly composed landscape painting, the opening opposite frames a view out to the Temple of Apollo high above the lake. Facing the exit from the Grotto is a lead statue of a classical river god, cast by Henry Cheere in 1751. He symbolises the river Stour and with his outstretched arm urges you on towards the Pantheon, the climax of your tour.

Between the Grotto and the Gothic Cottage is a fine example of the Cut-leaf Beech (*Fagus sylvatica* 'Aspleniifolia'), its leaves contrasting well with those of the Common Beech nearby. Common Beech is the dominant woodland tree in most of the views.

The Gothic Cottage

In 1763 Henry Hoare paid a visit to Horace Walpole's Gothick house at Strawberry Hill, which may have inspired him to introduce this quaint little rustic building. However, it remained hidden by vegetation during his time, and it was not until Richard Colt Hoare added the Gothic seat and porch in 1806 that it became a feature.

At this point, a clearing opens up to offer stunning views across the lake towards the village, and a sudden close-up view of the Pantheon, which was last seen from the south side of the lake.

The domed central chamber of the Grotto was built from brick, and then lined with rough limestone and Italian tufa to resemble a natural cave

The Gothic Cottage

13

'Pantheon' means a temple sacred to all the gods, and the interior of the Stourhead Pantheon is filled with statues of classical deities, including Hercules in the central niche. Painting by Samuel Woodforde, 1784

(*Right*) Diana the huntress, inside the Pantheon

The view from the Pantheon

The Pantheon

This is the largest and most important garden building at Stourhead, the focus of the main views, and an agreeable resting-place halfway round the circuit. It was originally heated by a stove at the back and would probably have been used by Henry Hoare II for picnics and supper parties. Built by Flitcroft in 1753–4, it was directly inspired by the Pantheon in Rome, one of the best preserved and most admired survivals of classical antiquity.

In the niches flanking the portico are statues of Bacchus, god of wine and rescuer of Ariadne (see p.13), and of Callipygian Venus. The 'Venus of the beautiful buttocks' recalls the legend of two sisters who could not agree who had the prettiest bottom. Finally, they asked a passerby to decide. The winner asked him to marry her, but honour was satisfied when his brother preferred the other sister and married her.

The interior is dominated by Michael Rysbrack's marble statue of Hercules, which was installed in 1757. Hercules had been associated with gardens since Roman times. Rysbrack based the figure both on the Farnese Hercules (a famous classical statue in Naples), but also on studies from life. The bulging biceps belonged to Jack Broughton, a Thames waterman who became a very successful prize-fighter and went on to run his own boxing stadium in London. In contrast, the pose – crossed legs and hand on hip – symbolised genteel elegance at the time. Walpole thought Rysbrack's statue 'an exquisite summary of his skill, knowledge and judgment'.

The other statues depict, from left to right, St Susanna (Henry Hoare II's wife and daughter were both called Susanna); Diana, goddess of hunting (a passion of his youth); Flora, goddess of gardens; Livia Augusta, wife of the Emperor Augustus and patron of Virgil; Meleager, lover of another huntress, Atalanta; and Isis, an Egyptian goddess also worshipped by the Romans.

The Pantheon: 'Few buildings exceed the magnificence, taste and beauty of this temple' (Horace Walpole, 1762)

The Iron Bridge

The bridge was built in 1860 to replace an earlier wooden bridge which provided a short cut across a narrow tongue of water sticking out from the north end of the lake.

The Dam and Cascade

The apparently natural lake that forms the hub of the garden was in fact a highly artificial creation, the result of an earth dam, which was built around 1754 across the western end of the valley. No attempt was made to disguise the dam's artificiality; indeed, it was always kept bare of planting on the lake side.

The cascade was added in 1766 as a decorative way of carrying surplus water from the main lake down to the lower pond in Turner's Paddock. It was designed with the help of Henry Hoare II's friend Copplestone Warre Bampfylde, who had designed a similar cascade in his own garden at Hestercombe in Somerset. Bampfylde's watercolours of Stourhead are illustrated on p.3 and 25.

Turn right over the Rock Arch to walk up to the Temple of Apollo, or carry straight on to the Bristol High Cross and the village. It is this choice – between the demanding, but rewarding, path and the easy, but less satisfying, one – that is represented symbolically in Poussin's Choice of Hercules which is on display with Henry Hoare II's collection in the house (illustrated on the right).

The Rock Arch

The arch is a decorative incident in the circuit walk, but was not meant to be seen from a distance. Since 1765 it has provided a bridge over the Zeals road, which was carefully sunk and lined with shrubs so that it would also be invisible from the garden.

Which way to turn? Hercules ponders whether to take the stony, uphill path of virtue (on the left) or the easier 'primrose path' of pleasure

The view from the dam towards the south side of the lake. Watercolour by Francis Nicholson, about 1813

(*Opposite*) The cascade was inspired by that at Hestercombe, the garden of Henry Hoare II's friend, Coplestone Warre Bampfylde. Painting by John Inigo Richards

The Temple of Apollo

High on a hill at the western end of the garden stands a circular temple dedicated to Apollo, the sun god who dwelt on Mount Parnassus and without whom no garden can flourish. He was originally represented inside by a copy of the Apollo Belvedere, perhaps the most revered of all classical statues, which also forms the focus of the Belvedere gardens in the Vatican. The temple was built by Flitcroft in 1765 to outdo William Chambers's slightly earlier Temple of the Sun at Kew, which was also based on a famous circular temple at Baalbec in Syria. As Joseph Spence remarked that same year: 'From it you take in all the chief beauties of the place ... when you walk round the [lake] ... you are almost continually entertain'd by the reflection of it in the water.'

Richard Colt Hoare was dissatisfied with its surroundings, as he explained in 1834, 'seated on a hill [it] presented a naked appearance, having only a smooth surface of turf. This hill has since been planted with forest trees and an underwood of laurel, which has greatly added to the rich appearance of the hill.' The lakeside below still supports a large number of fine specimen trees and shrubs, especially conifers and magnolias. There is another large Tulip Tree on the island in the centre of the view.

Walk back down the hill to rejoin the main path towards the village.

The Temple of Apollo was inspired by a circular temple at Baalbec, illustrated in Robert Wood's 1757 book on the classical ruins there. Henry Hoare II owned a copy

The panoramic view from the Temple of Apollo down over the lake (view I)

(*Right*) The Temple of Apollo

The Palladian Bridge

Henry Hoare II's first commission from Michael Rysbrack, in 1727, was for a bust of the 16th-century Italian architect Andrea Palladio. For early 18th-century men of taste like Hoare, Palladio was the supreme designer. His buildings inspired not only Stourhead House and a host of other country houses, but also a series of bridges in the great landscape gardens of the period. That at Stourhead was based on a Palladio bridge in Vicenza and is comparatively simple: a five-arched, slightly curved span. The Palladian Bridge provided an essential element in the middle ground of the carefully composed views to and from the Pantheon. But although it is purely ornamental, it was meant to look practical, as Henry Hoare explained in 1762: 'When you stand at the Pantheon the water will be seen thro the arches and it will look as if the river came down through the village and that this was the village bridge for publick use.'

The Bristol High Cross

This much-restored medieval monument originally stood at the junction of High Street and Broad Street in Bristol. It was removed as 'a ruinous and superstitious Relick, which is at present a public nuisance', and in 1764 was acquired by Henry Hoare II, who rebuilt it here the following year. Like the obelisk, it provided a useful vertical accent in the views, and it also sat easily beside the ancient Gothic church and the village, telling 'a tale of

other times', as the writer William Hazlitt put it.

The sculptures represent English monarchs: on the upper tier, Henry VI, Elizabeth I, James I and Charles I, and, on the lower tier, John, Henry II and Edward I (who, oddly, is included twice). They are replicas of the sadly eroded originals, which are now on show in the Victoria & Albert Museum in London. Hoare decided to paint their drapery red, blue and gold. The effect delighted his grandchildren, but Mrs Lybbe Powys, who visited in 1776, was less impressed, thinking that they would have 'looked better off the original colour than so ornamented ...; but still 'tis pretty through this profusion of finery'.

Stourton village

Many 18th-century landowners demolished ancient villages that got in the way of their gardening schemes. Henry Hoare realised that incorporating Stourton village into the garden would enhance the picturesque effect he wanted to achieve. Richard Colt Hoare thought that that he could make it more picturesque still in 1812 by pulling down cottages that would interfere with the views between the church and the garden.

St Peter's church

Here are buried Henry Hoare I and II, and Richard Colt Hoare and his wife Hester, who died young. There is also a monument to Henry II's steward Francis Faugoin, who supervised all the work in the garden.

The Palladian Bridge, with the Pantheon in the background (view J)

The garden from Stourton village in the early 19th century

The Bristol High Cross and St Peter's church, above a bank of rhododendrons and gunnera

The Wider Landscape

The garden lies at the heart of a traditional estate of over 1,000 hectares. It comprises fertile agricultural land, unimproved chalk downland and ancient woods, which are rich in wildlife and the remains of prehistoric hill-forts and burial mounds. A separate leaflet describes walks over the estate.

(*Opposite*) The Stourhead estate about 1813. Alfred's Tower can be seen on the horizon

Alfred's Tower

This triangular tower stands on Kingsettle Hill two miles north-west of the garden, on the spot where in 879 King Alfred raised his standard after emerging from hiding on the Isle of Athelney – the low point of his career. He went on to defeat the invading Danes at the battle of Eddington.

The statue of Alfred over the entrance bears an inscription written by Henry Hoare II, which describes him as:

> … the light of a benighted age
> … a Philosopher and Christian
> The Father of his People
> The Founder of the English
> Monarchy and Liberty.

Henry Hoare II decided to build the tower after reading the French thinker Voltaire's praise of Alfred. He also wanted to outdo his friend Charles Hamilton, who was planning something similar for his garden at Painshill. The tower commemorates the accession of George III in 1760 and the end of the Seven Years War three years later. It was the last work designed for Henry Hoare II by Henry Flitcroft, who died before it was completed. Unlike the other Stourhead monuments, it was constructed of brick, and the interior is hollow and unroofed. It was not meant to be lived in, but as the culmination of a ride from Six Wells Bottom. A spiral staircase takes you to a viewing platform at the top, from which you enjoy spectacular views over three counties.

In August 1944 the tower was hit by an American aircraft, killing the crew and dislodging the top ten metres, which have since been rebuilt.

The Makers of the Garden

Henry Hoare I, with a plan of the house he built at Stourhead

Origins

Stourton village was the home of the Stourton family from before the Norman Conquest. In 1448 Sir John Stourton enclosed 1,000 acres to make a park, and at some later point the stream through the valley was dammed to create a series of fish ponds. By 1704, when the bankrupt Stourtons were forced to sell up, Stourhead was said to have 'all the advantages of Fine Gardens, Orchards, Grove, Park'.

'Good' Henry Hoare I (1677–1725)

In 1717 the estate was bought for £14,000 by Henry Hoare, a prosperous second-generation banker from London. (The bank still trades from the same address – the Sign of the Golden Bottle, Fleet Street.) Most of his customers were country landowners, and he realised that they would be happier depositing their money with one of their own kind. A change in interest rates also made land a better investment than government securities. Hoare pulled down the old house and commissioned Colen Campbell to replace it with one of the first country houses in the Palladian style. To the east of the house was a railed forecourt with an oval lawn, and to the south were walled gardens.

Henry Hoare II 'the Magnificent' (1705–85)

'Good' Henry's son, another Henry, inherited in 1725 at the age of twenty, but for the next 20 years he did little at Stourhead, which remained his mother's home. As a young man, he had been bored by banking, spending much of his time staring out of the window, when he was not hunting or drinking. But, gradually, he applied himself, and by the mid-18th century he was the senior partner in the firm, which earned him £4,000 a year – a huge sum at the time.

Around 1733 he began extending his father's pleasure ground with a formal terrace walk of Scotch firs to the west of the house. At this point, the landscape below was still unplanted – 'naked hills and dreary valleys', as Mrs Lybbe Powys called it. In 1738 Henry went abroad, and 'the study of the fine arts occupied that attention in Italy which the pursuit of the fox had done in England'. When his mother died in 1741, he returned home to Stourhead. Two years later, his second wife, Susanna, also died, and it was only then that he set about applying what he had learned in Italy to the garden. His first garden building was the Temple of Flora, which was put up in 1744–6 by Henry Flitcroft in the same Palladian style as his father's house. Hoare relied on Flitcroft for all his later buildings, but seems to have trusted his own judgement when laying out the garden. In March 1752 his only son died of smallpox while on the Grand Tour in Naples. Shattered by this blow, Hoare stopped work on the garden for awhile.

Henry Hoare's masterstroke was the dam across the western end of the valley, which turned the series of fish-ponds into a single sheet of water. Around the new lake, he conceived an anti-clockwise circuit walk, which linked garden buildings and picturesque views in a carefully contrived sequence. The climax of the walk and views is the Pantheon, which was completed by 1757. The garden soon began to attract visitors like Horace Walpole, who was duly impressed, when he walked round in 1762: 'The whole composes one of the most picturesque scenes in the world.' The Temple of Apollo and the Bristol High Cross followed shortly afterwards, by which time the basic structure of the garden as we see it today was complete. Hoare lived 'to enjoy the gratifying sight of a desert converted into a paradise'. A team of 50 gardeners, supervised by the steward, Francis Faugoin, were kept busy looking after the garden. The whole project is thought to have cost Hoare over £20,000.

In his 70s, Hoare liked nothing better than showing the garden to his grandchildren: 'Thank God they are all fine and well, and now make nothing of walking round the gardens; and I mounted the [Alfred's] Tower Thursday with the dear children. The Temple of the Nymph [the Grotto] is all enchantment to them.' But his last years were darkened by the war in America, and by the worsening political situation at home. He feared that the whole financial system would collapse, bringing down Hoare's Bank with it. He was also haunted by the memory of his schoolfriend Charles Hamilton, who in 1773 had been forced by his creditors to sell off the famous landscape garden he had created at Painshill. So when Hoare handed over Stourhead to his grandson Richard Colt Hoare, he stipulated that Colt must sever all links with the family bank.

Planting
After laying out the Fir Walk in the 1730s, Hoare seems to have done little planting in the bare valley below till about 1750, when he 'proceeded *con spirito* upon a widely extended scale', according to his grandson.

He placed trees and shrubs just as he did his temples, to create pictorial effects, as he explained: 'The greens should be ranged together in large masses as the shades are in painting: to contrast the *dark* masses with *light* ones, and to relieve each dark mass itself with little sprinklings of lighter greens here and there.' He planted the slopes to the north and south of the lake with a mixture of broad-leaf species (beech, oak, field maple, sycamore, Spanish Chestnut, ash, holm oak) and conifers (larch, Norway Spruce, yew, Cedar of Lebanon). Weeping willow was concentrated by the shore near the Grotto, and Common Laurel was used throughout as underplanting.

Henry Hoare II, who conceived the garden

Henry Hoare II's garden in its prime. Watercolour by his friend, Coplestone Warre Bampfylde, about 1775

Richard Colt Hoare, with his son Henry, who died young

Pelargonium peltatum was one of many varieties grown at Stourhead by Colt Hoare that have recently been reintroduced by the National Trust

Sir Richard Colt Hoare (1758–1838)

Colt Hoare was a very different man from his grandfather – a quiet scholar rather than an extrovert businessman. As a child, he had spent his summer holidays at Stourhead, which he inherited in 1783 on his marriage to Hester Lyttelton of Hagley Hall. He was devastated by her death only two years later, and to try and get over his loss, he travelled abroad for the next six years, leaving Stourhead in the hands of his steward. He became fascinated by the landscapes of Italy, which he recorded in hundreds of highly accomplished drawings. In 1791 he was forced to return home by political upheavals on the Continent.

The wealth Colt Hoare inherited from his father and grandfather enabled him to pursue his antiquarian interests, which focussed on the prehistory of his native Wiltshire, and to develop the garden within the framework laid out by Henry Hoare II. He looked at Stourhead with the eyes of a practised landscape painter, naturalising the formal planting round the house and extending the park. He disliked 'nature overcrowded with buildings', and so removed various of the smaller structures round the lake, including the Turkish Tent, the Venetian Seat, a 'greenhouse of false Gothic', the Chinese Alcove and a wooden Palladian seat. He preferred the picturesque quality of the Gothic Cottage, which became a feature, to the smoothness of the classical temples. He also put down gravel paths, which made it easier to walk round the garden and formalised the circular route, which now started from the village rather than from the house. Defining the paths also enabled him to thicken the planting on either side.

Planting

Colt Hoare introduced the invasive *Rhododendron ponticum*. Many of these were later replaced by better hybrids, which now make such a spectacular display in spring. He planted ornamental shrubs to the south of the lake, and laurels on the slopes below the Temple of Apollo. He also thinned out his grandfather's firs, which he disliked, replacing them with more broad-leaved species, especially beech, together with acers, chestnuts, Tulip Trees, planes and limes. By 1810 one visitor felt that the planting was getting out of hand: 'The lawns are half-covered and belittled by shrubs, planted everywhere, particularly endless tufts and thickets of laurel; beautiful in themselves, but in too great profusion.' Colt was a knowledgeable plantsman, who was keen on the exotic new introductions which became fashionable in the early 19th century. He bred geraniums and hybrid pelargoniums in a conservatory (now gone) next to his new library. His last major alteration to the garden was to dig a new fourteen-acre lake below the dam, which was named Gaspar, after one of his favourite landscape painters, Gaspar Dughet.

Colt Hoare never remarried, and, crippled by gout and rheumatism, he spent most of his later years alone in his beloved library at Stourhead.

The Gothic Cottage, about 1813. Colt Hoare kept the large garden staff busy sweeping the gravel paths he had introduced. Watercolour by Francis Nicholson

The Victorians (1838–94)

Colt Hoare's half-brother, Henry Hugh, was already in his 70s, when he inherited Stourhead in 1838. He had only three years left to him to enjoy the place, but he re-established the connection between the garden and the Bank, which paid for rebuilding the obelisk and adding the portico to the house.

His son, Hugh Richard, was also a partner in the Bank, but retired from business as soon as he inherited in 1845. He concentrated his efforts on the estate rather than the garden, modernising many of the farm buildings and cottages. His great passion was for the Stourhead woods, which he renewed with new plantings of Scotch Fir, larch and spruce that would earn their keep as commercial forestry. In the garden, he planted some of the ornamental conifers that had recently been discovered in the Americas and Asia: Douglas Fir, Hemlock Spruce, Monkey Puzzle, and Lawson's Cypress. His Western Red Cedars and Coast Redwoods now dwarf the rest of the woods.

His nephew, Henry Ainslie Hoare, 5th Bt, spent part of his honeymoon at Stourhead, but really preferred a more social life in London and Paris. Growing increasingly short of money, he closed up the house after 1886, but he would still occasionally return to walk round the garden with his grandchildren and picnic at Alfred's Tower.

Hugh Richard Hoare, 4th Bt, who introduced many of the ornamental conifers in the garden

Augusta East, wife of the 5th Baronet, whose gambling debts forced them to live away from Stourhead in their later years

The garden in the late 19th century

The 20th Century

Sir Henry Hoare, 6th Bt brought a breath of new life to Stourhead, when he inherited in 1894. Like Colt Hoare, he did not work in the Bank, but lived the life of a country gentleman, breeding horses and cherishing the garden. James Lees-Milne described him a 'bluff John Bullish figure in his unvarying pepper-and-salt knickerbockers winter and summer, and fawn billycock (he is the only man I ever saw wearing a hat at luncheon). He was impatient and a little alarming, but astute and nice, and absolutely dedicated to Stourhead.'

After a decade of neglect, the garden was in a sad state: the Bristol High Cross was tottering on its foundations, and rampant laurel and rhododendron threatened to bring down the roof of the Grotto. Sir Henry set to work clearing the undergrowth and replanting with new kinds of ornamental trees and flowering shrubs. He was particularly fond of the more exotic hybrid rhododendrons with which from 1922 he replaced the ubiquitous *ponticum*. A large and dedicated garden staff kept everything in order.

Disaster and family tragedy overshadowed the 6th Baronet's life: in 1902 the core of the house was devastated by fire; worse followed in 1917, when his only son Henry died of his wounds while fighting in Egypt. Henry's name was never to be mentioned again in his presence. Like Colt Hoare, he suffered from rheumatism in old age, but still insisted on being taken round the garden in his wheelchair. Without an heir, he decided to give Stourhead to the National Trust in 1936 – the first property to be offered under the new Country Houses Scheme. The legal niceties were finally settled in 1946, the year before he died; his devoted wife, Alda, followed him only six hours later.

Sir Henry Hoare, 6th Bt, who revived the garden and bequeathed it to the National Trust

The 6th Baronet planted the ornamental acers, which turn a flaming red in autumn

The National Trust

In its first years in charge of Stourhead, the Trust concentrated on the woodland, removing dangerous and decrepit trees to ensure the long-term survival of the rest. The task was complicated in 1953 by a gale which brought down many of the mature beeches, oaks, chestnuts and larches. In the 1960s grants from the Historic Buildings Council enabled the Trust to repair the dam, the Rock Arch and the roof of the Temple of Apollo.

In 1978 the Trust published a Conservation Plan, which, for the first time, made proposals for the long-term management of the garden that were based on detailed historical research and recording of the surviving plant stock and buildings. The Plan spelt out four broad principles:

- Where Henry Hoare the Magnificent's creations survive (the circuit walk, the garden buildings and the views), they should be respected.
- Replanting should follow precedent.
- The garden round the lake should be allowed to merge gently into the more pastoral character of the wider landscape at Six Wells Bottom and below the dam.
- Replanting should aim at simplicity, rather than striking variety, of colour and shape (so, around the lake, unified masses of shrubs should be balanced with open areas of grass).

These principles have enabled Stourhead to change (as every garden must), while retaining the magical, intangible spirit that has made it a paradise on earth for more than two and a half centuries.

Alda, Lady Hoare, wife of the 6th Baronet. She was 'tall, upright and tightly corseted', according to James Lees-Milne

The crumbling Bristol High Cross needed careful restoration in 1979–81

(*Left*) The Pantheon from the south bank of the lake

31